WAC

Witness to History

The Vietnam War

www.heinemann.co.uk/library

Visit our website to find out more information about **Heinemann Library** books.

To order:
☎ Phone 44 (0) 1865 888066
▤ Send a fax to 44 (0) 1865 314091
▢ Visit the Heinemann Bookshop at www.heinemann.co.uk/library to browse our catalogue and order online.

First published in Great Britain by Heinemann Library,
Halley Court, Jordan Hill, Oxford
OX2 8EJ, part of Harcourt Education.

Heinemann is a registered trademark of
Harcourt Education Ltd.

Produced for **Heinemann** by Discovery Books Ltd
Editorial: Nancy Dickmann, Christine Lawrie and
    Tanvi Rai
Design: Ian Winton
Picture Research: Rachel Tisdale
Production: Séverine Ribierre

Originated by Dot Gradations
Printed and bound in China
by South China Printing Company

ISBN 0 431 17054 1 (hardback)
08 07 06 05 04
10 9 8 7 6 5 4 3 2 1

ISBN 0 431 17059 2 (paperback)
09 08 07 06
10 9 8 7 6 5 4 3 2 1

British Library Cataloguing in Publication Data
Burgan, Michael, 1960-
    The Vietnam War. – (Witness to History)
    959.7'043

A full catalogue record for this book is available from
the British Library.

Acknowledgements
The publishers would like to thank the following for
permission to reproduce photographs:
Bettmann/CORBIS pp. **8, 12, 14, 17, 18, 19, 20, 21, 24,
26, 32, 34, 35, 36, 40, 42, 48**; Bob Rowan; Progressive
Image/CORBIS p. **47**; CORBIS SYGMA p.**33**; Francoise
de Mulder/CORBIS p. **46**; Gideon Mendel/CORBIS
p. **49**; Hulton-Deutsch Collection/CORBIS p.**7**; Nik
Wheeler/CORBIS p. **44**; Peter Newark's Military
Pictures p. **31**; Popperphoto pp. **25, 38, 51**; Steve
Raymer/CORBIS p. **43**; Tim Page/CORBIS p. **28**;
TophamPicturepoint
pp. **4, 5, 10, 16, 22**.

Cover photograph shows a war photographer working
alongside US soldiers in South Vietnam recording his
experiences, reproduced with permission of
Bettmann/CORBIS.

The publishers would like to thank Bob Rees, historian
and assistant head teacher, for his assistance in the
preparation of this book.

Every effort has been made to contact copyright hold-
ers of any material reproduced in this book. Any omis-
sions will be rectified in subsequent printings if notice is
given to the publishers.

The paper used to print this book comes from
sustainable resources.

Words appearing in the text in bold, **like this**, are explained in the glossary.

Contents

Introduction

For almost 30 years, the USA tried to influence events in Vietnam, a small Asian nation more than 11,000 kilometres (7000 miles) from its Pacific coast. The US interest in Vietnamese affairs led to the Vietnam War (1959-1975), one of the most devastating conflicts of the 20th century. The long war killed about 1 million soldiers, most of them Vietnamese. Several million civilians also died, and the fighting spread beyond Vietnam to the neighbouring countries of Cambodia and Laos.

As the Vietnam War progressed, it led many Americans in the USA to question their government and its policies. Some people around the world said the war was immoral, as the USA was not directly threatened by Vietnam. They felt that a large, powerful nation was killing innocent people for its own selfish ends. Others, however, said the USA did have a valid reason for fighting in Vietnam: to stop the spread of what it considered to be an evil political system, **communism**.

Path to war

At the end of World War II (1939-1945), a group of Vietnamese communists led by Ho Chi Minh declared Vietnam's independence from France. The US government gave France financial aid as it fought to keep control of Vietnam. This first Vietnam War ended in 1954, with Ho's victory forcing the French out of **Indochina**. The war, however, left Vietnam split. Ho and the communists controlled the north, while a pro-American, anti-communist government ruled the south. Ho, still seeking a unified Vietnam, aided communists in the south. These Vietnamese were known as the **Viet Cong**. In 1959, the North Vietnamese government officially approved using force in the south to achieve its political goals.

Wearing traditional peasant clothes, Viet Cong **guerrillas** search for enemy forces. Vietnam was largely a poor, agricultural country when the war began.

On a search-and-destroy mission, a US soldier destroys a hut, part of a camp used by the Viet Cong.

The USA supported Ngo Dinh Diem, South Vietnam's leader at the time, sending him money, arms and military advisers. Starting in 1961, President John F. Kennedy increased the number of advisers. About 16,000 served in Vietnam by the time of his **assassination** in November 1963. Less than two years later, President Lyndon Johnson sent the first US combat troops to fight the Viet Cong and the North Vietnamese soldiers who were helping them. By 1969, more than 500,000 US troops were fighting in Vietnam.

Starting in 1969, under President Richard Nixon, the USA pursued a new policy. Facing growing criticism of the war, Nixon pulled out US troops while equipping its South Vietnamese **allies** so they could continue the fighting. Nixon also increased US military activity in Laos and Cambodia, hoping to limit North Vietnamese activity in those countries. At the same time, the USA and North Vietnam held peace talks. In January 1973, the two sides reached an agreement, and the last US combat troops soon left Vietnam. The war, however, continued for two more years – North Vietnam against South Vietnam. In the end, the North Vietnamese won, creating a single communist state.

How do we know?

The Vietnam War has been called a 'television war'. For the first time in history, people around the world could turn on their TV sets and see daily reports on the fighting. Some historians think that seeing the horrors of war so vividly while sitting in their homes increased the opposition of many Americans to the war. Vietnam also attracted international journalists and photographers who roamed the battlefields and villages, trying to uncover the truth about the fighting. About 75 journalists from all types of media died covering the Vietnam War.

Newspapers and television reports are two examples of primary sources. They provide direct evidence of what was said and done during the Vietnam War. Other primary sources include government documents, the later writings of government officials, and oral (spoken) histories – personal accounts from people who were there at the time. A number of oral histories provide the views of soldiers and civilians from both sides of the war.

Primary sources are used by historians and scholars to create secondary sources – books, articles and documentaries that describe and interpret the war. Good secondary sources are factually accurate, but they still reflect the attitudes and beliefs of the people who create them. Sometimes a variety of primary and secondary sources, taken together, provide the most balanced view of a topic. Secondary sources are only as good as the primary sources they are based on, and a primary source might provide a distorted view of the truth. One person's experiences on a war front, for instance, gives only a small part of the overall picture. People speaking or writing long after the war might forget how something actually happened. Personal accounts are also coloured by the opinions of the people recollecting events. The people involved might also lie about their actions, to cover up a mistake or take credit for something they didn't do.

New sources emerge

Primary sources from governments provide useful information on official polices. Government sources, however, are no more objective than personal accounts. And at times, governments keep some information **classified**. This process prevents an enemy – or their own citizens – from learning the truth about sensitive issues. The US government kept many documents classified during the Vietnam War. Over time, the government has **declassified** some of them, shedding new light on certain issues. New primary sources also come from Vietnam and its wartime **allies** the Soviet Union and China. In 1991, **communism** ended in the Soviet Union and the government was replaced. Afterwards, new leaders allowed Western scholars to see some previously secret documents. The Chinese and Vietnamese have also opened up some of their **archives**, as they have developed better relations with the **West**. Still, all the governments that took part in the war keep some documents classified. Scholars might need decades to uncover all the facts about the Vietnam War.

In 1968, war photographers Larry Burrows and Terry Fincher take a break from the action. Journalists from both print and electronic media gave the world detailed accounts of the Vietnam War. Burrows was killed covering a South Vietnamese offensive in 1971.

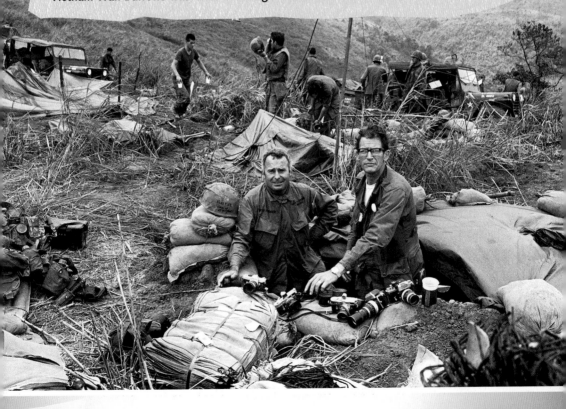

Colonial Vietnam

In 111 BC, China invaded Vietnam. The Chinese ruled there for more than 1000 years, until the mid-10th century, when the Vietnamese finally forced them out and established an independent kingdom. That independence lasted until 1862, when the Vietnamese emperor Tu Duc gave control of part of his country to France. In the 19th century, France, like other European nations, wanted **colonies** in Asia. The French slowly extended their control over the rest of Vietnam and neighbouring Laos and Cambodia, creating what was called French **Indochina**.

Under French rule, Vietnamese **nationalism** began to develop. During the 1920s and 1930s a young nationalist and **communist** named Ho Chi Minh led the resistance to the French. When World War II began, Japan invaded Vietnam. During the war, the French government came under German control, and it worked with the Japanese in

In 1862, the French gained control of Cochin China, part of Vietnam. By 1893 they had taken over the whole region.

Indochina. Ho decided the Vietnamese should fight both colonial powers: France and Japan. Ho and other communists formed the *Viet Nam Doc Lap Minh* – the Vietnam Independence League. Known as the Viet Minh, this group battled against the Japanese and the French throughout the war. On 2 September 1945, Japan surrendered to the USA, Great Britain and their **allies**. The same day, Ho Chi Minh announced the creation of a new independent country: the **Democratic Republic** of Vietnam.

Ho Chi Minh founded Vietnam's Communist Party in 1930. He led the party until his death in 1969.

Declaration of independence

When he announced his country's independence, Ho Chi Minh deliberately drew on the wording of the American Declaration of Independence, in which the American colonies declared their independence from the British Empire. Here is part of his declaration of independence for Vietnam.

All men are created equal; they are endowed [given] by their Creator with certain unalienable Rights [rights that cannot be taken away]; among these are Life, Liberty, and the pursuit of Happiness.

This immortal [endlessly important] statement was made in the Declaration of Independence of the United States of America in 1776. In a broader sense, this means: All the peoples on the earth are equal from birth, all the peoples have a right to live, to be happy and free.

The Declaration of the French Revolution made in 1791 on the Rights of Man and the Citizen also states: 'All men are born free and with equal rights, and must always remain free and have equal rights.'

Those are undeniable truths.

*Nevertheless, for more than eighty years, the French **imperialists**, abusing the standard of Liberty, Equality, and Fraternity, have violated [treated with disrespect] our Fatherland and oppressed our fellow citizens. They have acted contrary to the ideals of humanity and justice…*

After the Japanese had surrendered to the Allies, our whole people rose to regain our national sovereignty and to found the Democratic Republic of Viet-Nam…

The whole Vietnamese people, animated [made active] by a common purpose, are determined to fight to the bitter end against any attempt by the French colonialists to reconquer their country.

The French War

Around the world, many **colonized** people hoped the end of World War II would lead to their independence. France did grant independence to some of its former colonies, such as Syria and Lebanon, but French leaders considered **Indochina** too valuable to give up. They ignored Ho's declaration of independence, though they signed an agreement with the Viet Minh in March 1946 that would make Vietnam a so-called 'free state' within France's empire. French troops would stay in Vietnam, although the Vietnamese would run the local government and have their own army. The two sides, however, began fighting before they worked out the details of this agreement.

In November 1946, Viet Minh and French forces clashed in Haiphong. The French then bombarded the city, killing more than 6000 people. The next month, Ho's forces attacked the French, starting a war that would last for almost eight years. Ho had hoped the USA would recognize his country's independence. President Harry Truman, however, wanted to restore French rule in Vietnam. American leaders wanted French support for their international policies and they distrusted Ho's **communist** background (see page 12).

Medical workers carry a French soldier wounded at Dien Bien Phu in May 1954. About 2000 French troops were killed and thousands more were taken prisoner, out of a force of about 16,000.

Starting in 1950, the USA sent money and supplies to the French. By 1954, the Americans were paying for almost 80 per cent of the war effort. Still, the Vietnamese fought on, and in May 1954 General Vo Nguyen Giap led them to victory at the battle of Dien Bien Phu. With their defeat, the French decided to pull out of Vietnam for good.

A soldier's experience
The battle at Dien Bien Phu was a six-week long **siege**. About 60,000 well-armed Viet Minh had taken control of the mountains surrounding the French camps there. In March 1954, they began to pound the French with **artillery** fire before finally taking control of the camps in May. Jean Pouget, a French soldier, describes his experience at Dien Bien Phu.

I arrived during the night of May 2, and Dien Bien Phu fell on May 7. The memory I keep of it is one block of time. There was no day or night. I never lay down. I never slept. I don't remember eating. At four o'clock in the morning there was a lull. We were 35 left at my post, with one machine gun, one grenade left... We built a barricade with corpses at the entrance since we had no sandbags, and we waited. And we saw the shadows coming one by one, the Viet Minh. I decided to throw my grenade and we immediately got return fire. One of my last impressions was to feel the wall of corpses shivering under the burst of fire. Then a grenade must have hit my helmet because the net was burned and the helmet dented. American helmets are very solid. I lost consciousness and when I came to, there was above me, very close, a surgeon's mask from which a voice came: 'You are a prisoner of the army of the **Democratic Republic of Vietnam.**'

Cold War conflict

The US interest in **Indochina** was shaped by the **Cold War**. This **ideological** battle between the **democratic-capitalist** USA (and its **allies**) and the **communist** Soviet Union (and its allies) began after World War II. The Soviet Union wanted to extend its influence around the world by supporting communist governments that it could then control. The USA sought to promote capitalism and democratic governments, while halting Soviet gains.

In the 1950s, communism seemed to be spreading rapidly. In 1949, communists led by Mao Zedong had taken control of China. Mao had received some aid from the Soviet Union, though he and Soviet leaders sometimes disagreed. The next year, the Soviets backed an invasion of South Korea (an ally of the USA) by communist North Korea. This began the Korean War (1950-1953). These two events convinced US leaders that the Soviet Union wanted to dominate Asia.

The military aid the USA gave France to fight the Viet Minh was part of the US strategy of containment, or stopping the spread of communism. In 1954, President Dwight D. Eisenhower talked about the 'domino theory': if one South-east Asian nation came under communist control, its neighbours would too. The countries were like dominoes lined up in a row – when one fell, the others would fall after them. The USA was determined to prevent Vietnam from falling to communism.

John Foster Dulles, left, and President Dwight Eisenhower shaped early US policies toward South-east Asia. Dulles served as US secretary of state from 1953 until 1959.

John Foster Dulles was President Eisenhower's secretary of state, advising him on foreign affairs. Dulles helped shape the US policy on Vietnam. On 29 March 1954, about a month before the fall of Dien Bien Phu, Dulles suggested that the USA might have to play a direct military role in Indochina. Here is part of his speech.

Recent statements have been designed to impress upon potential **aggressors** that aggression might lead to action at places and by means of free-world choosing, so that aggression would cost more than it could gain.

...Under all circumstances it seems desirable to clarify further the United States' position.

Under the conditions of today, the imposition in South-east Asia of the political system of Communist Russia and its Chinese Communist ally, by whatever means, would be a grave threat to the whole free community. The United States feels that that possibility should not be passively accepted but should be met by united action. This might involve serious risks. But these risks are far less than those that will face us a few years from now if we dare not be resolute today.

The free nations want peace. However, peace is not had merely by wanting it. Peace has to be worked for and planned for. Sometimes it is necessary to take risks to win peace just as it is necessary in war to take risks to win victory. The chances for peace are usually bettered by letting a potential aggressor know in advance where his aggression could lead him.

Two Vietnams

During the summer of 1954, French and Viet Minh leaders met in Geneva, Switzerland, to officially end their war. Joining them at this conference were representatives from several other countries with an interest in finding peace and influencing events in **Indochina**; these included China, the Soviet Union, Great Britain, and the USA. The agreement signed in Geneva split Vietnam at the **17th parallel** and created a **demilitarized zone** there. Ho and the Viet Minh controlled the country north of this line. In the south was the State of Vietnam, a pro-French, anti-**communist** government that opposed Ho. This situation was only meant to be temporary and, under the accords (agreements), all Vietnamese would choose the leaders of a unified government in 1956.

In 1954, Vietnam was divided into North and South at the 17th parallel. The map also shows important places mentioned in the book.

In the north, Ho began putting a communist system in place. His government killed many landowners and took their farms, a policy Viet Minh leaders later admitted was a mistake. Meanwhile, in the south, Ngo Dinh Diem emerged as the leader. Using violence and fraud, he won an election and founded the **Republic** of Vietnam (South Vietnam). Diem ignored the Geneva Conference's plans for nationwide elections. He was determined to rule a separate, non-communist Vietnam, and the USA openly supported him.

Viet Minh troops march into Hanoi after taking control of the city from the French in October 1954.

14

A child's experience

After the splitting of Vietnam, the Viet Minh tried to recruit South Vietnamese who were opposed to Diem. Here, Truong Mealy describes his experience with a **cadre**, a dedicated Viet Minh member who spread communism in the south.

I was ten years old when a Viet Minh convinced me to go to a secret school... I just followed their instructions. They had me distribute handwritten leaflets around the marketplace saying things about higher salaries and justice. And they asked me to introduce them to three of my friends: 'One becomes three; three becomes nine and this way we will have many people.'

...My teacher told me, 'Do you know why Ngo Dinh Diem came to Vietnam? He was sent by the US. Now his whole family has power and all the poor people must work to feed them. Who should run Vietnam - Diem or Ho Chi Minh?'

They never called themselves Communists during this time. But they said, 'The Vietnamese people want to have a free government. Nothing is better than independence and liberty. Our best friend is the Soviet Union. It took the United States a hundred years to have progress but in only forty years the Soviet Union has become prosperous. Why? Because the Americans are capitalists, a few people take power. But in the Soviet Union the power is in the hands of all the people.'

I said 'That's wonderful. Really wonderful.' And I tried to march along with them.

The advisers

To protect his government, Ngo Dinh Diem arrested and sometimes killed the Viet Minh (members of the Vietnam Independence League) and their supporters in South Vietnam. In 1959, Ho decided the Viet Minh should fight back, and they began a **guerrilla war** against Diem's forces. The **communist** fighters in the south were called the **Viet Cong** (VC). The next year, the North Vietnamese organized the National Liberation Front (NLF) in South Vietnam. This political group included non-communists who opposed Diem, but Ho and his aides (assistants) directed it as they pursued their goal of unification.

In January 1961, John F. Kennedy replaced Dwight Eisenhower as president of the USA. Eisenhower had sent 900 US military advisers to Vietnam to help Diem fight the Viet Cong. The advisers included US Special Forces – troops trained to fight with great secrecy behind enemy lines. The USA was also providing economic aid (money) to the South Vietnamese army, the ARVN (Army of the **Republic** of Vietnam). Kennedy, concerned about growing communist influence around the world, decided to increase the US commitment to South Vietnam. The president sent more money. He also sent helicopters and aircraft. US advisers flew these aircraft and sometimes helped the ARVN fight the Viet Cong. In public, however, the government downplayed the role US soldiers played in Vietnam and kept secret some of their activities.

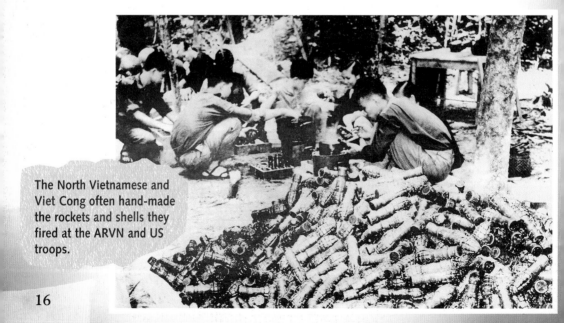

The North Vietnamese and Viet Cong often hand-made the rockets and shells they fired at the ARVN and US troops.

New York Times

Today American warships are helping the Vietnamese Navy to guard the sea frontier against infiltration from North Vietnam and U.S. Navy servicemen presently will arrive to help clean out guerrillas from the maze of tidal waterways in the Mekong River delta. The U.S. Army helicopter crews have come under fire taking Vietnamese combat troops into guerrilla zones or carrying pigs and other livestock to hungry outposts surrounded by hostile country. U.S. Air Force pilots have flown with Vietnamese pilots on bombing missions against reported enemy concentrations and against two frontier forts recently evacuated by the Vietnamese Army.

So far our contribution in blood has been small. One American sergeant has been killed by enemy action and another is missing and presumed captured. Inevitably, our casualties will grow.

...The United States seems... committed to a long, inconclusive war. The Communists can prolong it for years. Even without large-scale interventions from the North... what may be achieved at best is only a restoration of a tolerable security... But it is too late to disengage [pull out]; our prestige has been committed. Washington says we will stay until the finish.

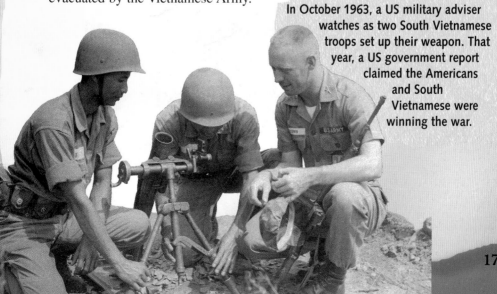

In October 1963, a US military adviser watches as two South Vietnamese troops set up their weapon. That year, a US government report claimed the Americans and South Vietnamese were winning the war.

Widening the war

The **assassination** of John F. Kennedy on 22 November 1963, thrust Vice President Lyndon B. Johnson into the White House. LBJ, as he was called, kept Kennedy's aides (advisers) and the commitment to prevent a **communist** takeover in South Vietnam. The war seemed to be going poorly. At times, US generals considered the use of **nuclear weapons** against North Vietnam. Some also suggested conventional bombing there and along the **Viet Cong** supply route from the north called the Ho Chi Minh Trail, which ran through parts of Cambodia and Laos. Johnson, however, was reluctant to pursue open, direct military involvement.

LBJ changed his mind in August 1964. That month, a US spy ship briefly came under attack in the Gulf of Tonkin, off the coast of North Vietnam. The US government later wrongly claimed that the North Vietnamese attacked a second time, and Johnson used that claim to put the Tonkin Gulf Resolution before the US **Congress**. If approved, this would give the president further powers to wage a wider war against North Vietnam. Congress did approve it.

By this time the US military was already carrying out secret missions in North Vietnam, blowing up bridges and other important targets. US planes were also bombing Viet Cong positions in Laos, along Vietnam's western border. The North Vietnamese had set up training camps there. Johnson soon ordered massive bombing raids on the North Vietnamese capital, Hanoi. And on 8 March 1965, the first 3500 US combat troops arrived in South Vietnam. The number grew to more than 180,000 by the end of 1965.

Lyndon Johnson was determined to stop the spread of communism, yet he was reluctant at first to increase the US military presence in South-east Asia.

Telling it like it is

US troops fought one of their first major ground battles of the Vietnam War at Ia Drang. The enemy included both Viet Cong and members of the North Vietnamese Army (NVA). Jack Smith was a private first class with the US 7th Cavalry. Here he recounts some of the sights and sounds of battle.

Nothing prepares you for combat. The best way to prepare a company for combat is to line the company up against a wall and fire a machine gun at them for about ten seconds. And tell the survivors, 'You're now combat-trained.' That's not pleasant, but that's what combat's like.

We walked in and we got into Landing Zone X-Ray on the third day of the battle there. It was just about over... I had never seen men as filthy as that... Their clothing was so covered with dirt, they looked like they were part of the dirt because they had been living in the dirt, living in foxholes for three days. They all had these thousand-yard stares that people talk about. The stare of someone who is nineteen years old but going on fifty, who has seen combat and been killing people and seen his friends killed under continuous bombardment, artillery and **napalm**, day in, day out. Stacks of dead bodies, stacks of wounded, equipment around the landing zone. And the one thing that sticks in my mind, there were bullets whizzing over the landing zone, humming like bees.

US Marines land at Da Nang, South Vietnam, in March 1965, as the USA commits itself to a full-scale war.

19

Friend or foe?

The **Viet Cong** (VC) used a variety of tactics to fight their **guerrilla war**. They hid in the rain forests and swamps, waiting to **ambush** enemy troops. They built simple traps in the ground filled with sharp sticks, called *punjis*, which were often tipped with poison. For weapons, the VC used captured US guns as well as arms sent from the Soviet Union and China. As the war went on, they also relied on military help from the North Vietnamese Army (NVA). Starting in 1964, these regular troops fought side-by-side with the VC.

In November 1965, a US soldier walks carefully through bamboo *punji* sticks. Viet Cong booby traps such as these struck about 28 per cent of the US forces killed or injured during combat.

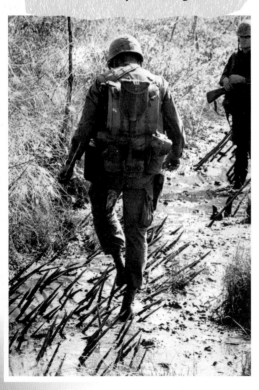

From the beginning of the Vietnam War, US troops struggled to distinguish the Viet Cong and their supporters from ordinary civilians. Viet Cong dressed as typical peasants and lived and worked in the villages the Americans patrolled. If US troops searched a village, the fighters fled, hiding in nearby rain forest or fields. The VC returned when the Americans left. US troops sometimes destroyed villages where suspected VC lived. Innocent people lost their homes – and sometimes their lives – in these raids. The Americans, however, felt they could not take chances, since many civilians were fighting for the Viet Cong. US soldiers could never be sure if the people they met had a bomb strapped to their body or a gun hidden in a farm cart.

Very few people betrayed us. That's why the Americans killed civilians...

Civilians were put in concentration camps. . . (see page 22). At night nobody was permitted to leave the camps. In the daytime, if the soldiers didn't think the

When entering South Vietnamese villages, US troops often had trouble telling friend from foe because Viet Cong guerrillas dressed as civilians.

people were going to help the Viet Cong, they let them go to the fields, to let them grow rice, potato, manioc.

...We had no weapons. The Americans and their coalition (**allies**) had very modern weapons - simple against modern, so we had to be clever. They didn't know that the VC surrounded their camps. We took unexploded bombs and shells, and made mines. We put them on the roads and destroyed their tanks. We saw where they were coming and mined those places. . . We made a huge mine, took a 200-litre can of petrol, filled it with explosives, connected it to a line and planted it on [a] hill. . . We saw a lot of smoke and American bodies flying in the air, and then we heard the explosion. Helicopters came and removed the bodies, but they left one. We bound him in cloth and buried him. Alive they were our enemies, but in death we were all human.

Methods of war

The USA often changed its strategy and tactics during the war. At first, the USA strengthened South Vietnam's defences, to prevent a possible attack from the north. Then, the Americans and South Vietnamese adapted to the **Viet Cong**'s **guerrilla warfare**. Part of their new strategy included building 'strategic hamlets'. Civilians were placed in guarded **stockades** so they could not aid the Viet Cong. But, the people hated being forced from their homes, so the programme was dropped.

When US ground troops arrived, they used a tactic called 'search and destroy' (see page 5). They hunted for VC camps and destroyed them or tried to catch the enemy in an **ambush**. The Viet Cong, however, were often able to slip away before the Americans could reach them. Against the NVA, US forces used **artillery** and received air support from planes and helicopters. The Americans also dropped chemicals such as Agent Orange. This **defoliant** killed trees and plants that the VC and NVA used to hide their movements. However, it also had side effects that still affect people today (see page 48).

The USA hoped massive bombing attacks in the north would break North Vietnam's will to continue the war. Using its huge B-52 bombers and other planes, the US military dropped more bombs during this war than both sides used during World War II.

Huge clouds of flames mark a napalm attack. Both sides used the chemical. The North Vietnamese fired it from handheld weapons called flamethrowers while the Americans dropped it as bombs from aircraft.

Report from an anti-war conference

In Vietnam, US planes often dropped **napalm** on their enemy. In 1971, panelists at an anti-war conference in Detroit, Michigan, described the impact of napalm on its victims.

PANELIST: In Dong Ha, located about 18 miles south of the **demilitarized zone**, they have a children's hospital. It's all Vietnamese children... They had a lot of children in there for treatment of diseases. There was one specific child I saw. I asked the child what had happened to him, and he said he'd been hit by napalm. His face, from his right eye around the back of his head (and had no ear), on down to the middle of his chest, was like one big mass of scar that'd just grown together. He'd been treated, but there's not a whole lot they can do for him. There's several of these cases, you know. I'm sure these people could tell you.

MODERATOR: Who else saw it? Anybody else see napalm?

DR. DAVID GALICIA: I saw the effects a couple of times. One I distinctly remember was a lady I used to see out in the yard in between two of the wards. This lady'd been burned beyond recognition, facial-wise. She had no face. Her eyes were left and they had somehow or another grafted some skin over the front of her head. She had some sort of an orifice left that she could take food through, but that's about it. She'd been the victim of napalm.

The South Vietnamese

The Vietnam War drastically changed daily life for the South Vietnamese – usually for the worse. A few people, particularly Buddhist monks, tried to protest against the war. Buddhists were a majority of the population in South Vietnam, but the country's leaders were Roman Catholics and denied them political power.

The largely Catholic government had many **corrupt** leaders. At times, they stole US aid meant to strengthen the military and the country's economy. South Vietnam never developed a true **democratic** government, despite holding elections during the mid-1960s.

The war had perhaps its greatest impact on the peasants of South Vietnam. To escape the fighting, thousands of rural South Vietnamese fled to the cities, where they lived in poverty. Those who stayed in their villages had to deal with the Viet Cong, who sometimes forced the peasants to provide food or hiding places. Some people, however, welcomed the Viet Cong, even though they had to pay them taxes and sacrifice some of their freedom. The **communists** seemed to offer more hope for a better future than their own corrupt leaders. And while the Americans talked of winning the 'hearts and minds' of the South Vietnamese, some US troops held racist attitudes toward them. They insulted the South Vietnamese, calling them 'gooks' and 'slopes' while raiding their villages and sometimes killing innocent people.

Buddhist monks demonstrating in Saigon, capital of South Vietnam, in 1966, demand the resignation of the president, Nguyen Van Thieu.

Coping with the Americans

Le Ly Hayslip was 12 years old when US troops first arrived in her village of Ky La, South Vietnam. In her autobiography *When Heaven and Earth Changed Places*, Hayslip described how she and her friends reacted to the Americans.

In 1966, a US marine visits a school in Da Nang, part of an American effort to win the support of South Vietnamese civilians.

In time, we all would learn the wisdom of standing still at the approach of Americans – the way one learns to stand still in the face of an angry dog. Before long, any Vietnamese who ran from American gunships would be considered Viet Cong and shot down for the crime of fear.

Although Americans had been in the village before and now came more frequently to Ky La, we children never got used to them. Because they had blue eyes and always wore sunglasses, a few of us thought they were blind. We called them mat meo – cat eyes – and 'long nose' to their backs and repeated every wild story we heard about them. Because the Viet Cong, when they captured them, always removed the Americans' boots (making escape too painful for their soft, citified feet), we thought we could immobilize the Americans by stealing both their sunglasses and their shoes. How can a soldier fight, we reasoned, if he's not only blind but lame?

Still, the arrival of the Americans in ever-increasing numbers meant the new war had expanded beyond anyone's wildest dreams. A period of great danger – one we couldn't imagine at the time – was about to begin.

Life during wartime

In North Vietnam, the people were united behind Ho Chi Minh, who was sometimes called 'Uncle Ho'. This was because most Northerners who opposed **communism** had already fled the country, been imprisoned, or been killed. The Communist Party controlled everything in the north, and citizens had to join if they wanted good jobs. Peasants and young soldiers learned communist philosophy, and North Vietnamese leaders stressed that the war was meant to free the south from American **imperialism**. Still, as the deaths mounted, some North Vietnamese did question the war, though rarely in public. Some young men tried to avoid the **draft** – just as many young Americans did.

US bombings disrupted life in the north. Food was scarce, and schools, factories and shops had to move from the cities to the countryside to escape the bombs. Civilians built bunkers, where they could seek protection during the raids. Hundreds of thousands of North Vietnamese also helped build and maintain the Ho Chi Minh Trail. Using mostly shovels and their hands, the North Vietnamese turned a simple rain forest path into a major supply highway. The trail had several different routes that stretched for a total of almost 16,000 km (10,000 miles).

The North Vietnamese used their own bicycles and Soviet-made trucks to move supplies along the Ho Chi Minh Trail.

As a teenager, Le Thanh eagerly joined the Communist Party in North Vietnam. He later left the country and moved to the USA. In this interview, Thanh describes life in the north during the war.

During the bombings everyone suffered. Hatred for Saigon [the South Vietnamese capital] and the Americans grew even stronger than it had before. A lot of young people volunteered for the army at that time.

But there was also a lot of anxiety. Everybody was excited by news about our great victories in the South and about the opposition movements that were fighting against the inhuman regime in Saigon. But there was no news from my friends who had gone South - nobody was hearing anything... So there was a lot of confusion about what was really going on and a lot of tension. When people would complain or ask questions they were criticized or arrested by the security police...

Nobody could get away from the war. It didn't matter if you were in the countryside or the city. While I was living in the country I saw terrible things... I saw children who had been killed, pagodas [Buddhist temples] and churches that had been destroyed, monks and priests dead in the ruins, schoolboys who were killed when their schools were bombed. When I saw these horrors my only feeling was that I wanted to kill Americans.

The media war

Reporters from around the world tried to capture the reality of the Vietnam War. As during past wars, print journalists covered battles and analysed the progress of the war. But for the first time ever, television also played a major part in reporting a foreign war. At first, US television networks limited their broadcast of combat scenes. Still, what they did show upset some US officials, who wanted to **censor** the television reporting. The images, they feared, would weaken public support for the war, and some historians say the broadcasts did have that effect.

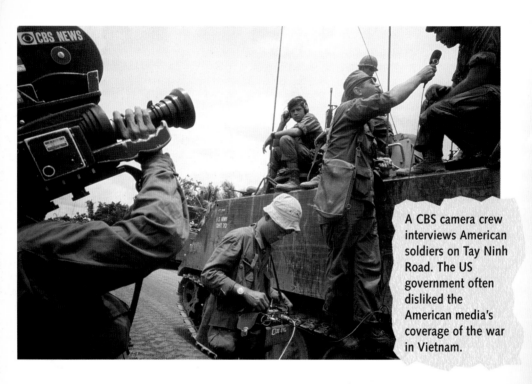

A CBS camera crew interviews American soldiers on Tay Ninh Road. The US government often disliked the American media's coverage of the war in Vietnam.

The journalists argued that they merely reported what they saw and heard – and told the truth when the government did not. Some journalists were openly against the war. Others began to oppose it only after seeing civilians killed or coming to the conclusion that the war could not be won. During the 1960s, Walter Cronkite was one of the most respected TV news figures in America. In 1968, he began to question the war. President Johnson realized that if Cronkite no longer supported him, many average Americans must feel the same way.

These briefings were much ridiculed, and there were many valid criticisms. But...for all their failings, the Follies were not the pack of lies that some critics suggested. The best reporters and news organizations recognized the value of an on-the-record, official version of events to compare with information from field reporters and other sources.

As important as it was to get the official version, there was no substitute for hands-on coverage, and reporters and photographers were always in the field. We drove down roads until the emptiness told us not to go any further. We trudged and sweated with the infantry and Marines, made harrowing helicopter assaults into landing zones, cowered behind paddy dikes as bullets cracked overhead. We waited long hours at isolated helicopter pads, saw B-52 strikes blossom like giant brown flowers, learned the culinary tricks of a C-ration [food for soldiers in the field], interviewed generals, lieutenants, sergeants and privates in their natural habitat, where the truth at least was bullet-proof.

Field officers and soldiers welcomed journalists; they wanted people at home to know what they were doing and enduring, and recognized our readiness to share their perils to tell their story.

Trouble at home

The **civil rights** movement was under way as the Vietnam War began. The movement's goal was to win legal equality for African-Americans. Civil rights leader Martin Luther King also spoke out against the war. He realized that the more money the US government spent on the war, the less it could spend to help poor people, which included many African-Americans. King also saw that a higher percentage of blacks and other minorities were serving on the front lines in Vietnam, compared to the percentage of **draft**-age whites. For the first years of the war, young men in college, who were more likely to be white, had received deferments, meaning they were not eligible for the draft.

As more Americans began to oppose the war, they adopted some of the methods of the civil rights movement, such as marches and non-violent **demonstrations**. The largest rallies drew hundreds of thousands of people. Some young men became draft-dodgers – they refused to report when chosen for military service. One of these was Muhammed Ali, the world heavyweight boxing champion who, because of his action, was stripped of his title. Such a famous name made people all over the world aware of the growing opposition to the war. Both President Johnson and Richard Nixon, who took over the presidency in 1969, thought the protesters were disloyal to their government.

The anti-war movement influenced popular culture. Musical groups sang songs against the war, and symbols of peace, such as two fingers raised in a V, appeared on posters and badges. During past wars, the US film industry had made movies that promoted the war effort. With rare exceptions, such as *The Green Berets*, starring John Wayne, film companies avoided making movies about Vietnam. They saw how split Americans were over fighting the war.

In 1917, Uncle Sam, a symbol of the USA, appeared on posters calling on Americans to help fight World War I with the slogan 'I Want You'. In 1971, Vietnam War protesters created this poster, showing a war-weary Sam with a different slogan.

An ex-soldier protests

Some soldiers returned from Vietnam thinking the US government had made a mistake by entering the war. In 1967, a group of them formed Vietnam Veterans Against the War (VVAW). Ron Kovic, who lost the use of his legs in Vietnam, joined VVAW. Here is a selection from his autobiography, *Born on the Fourth of July*.

I was in Vietnam when I first heard about the thousands of people protesting the war in the streets of America. I didn't want to believe it at first – people protesting against us when we were putting our lives on the line for our country. The men in my outfit used to talk about it a lot. How could they do this to us?...

But the hospital had changed all that. It was the end of whatever belief I'd still had in what I'd done in Vietnam. Now I wanted to know what I had lost my legs for, why I and the others had gone at all. But it was still very hard for me to think of speaking out against the war, to think of joining those I'd once called traitors...

I WANT OUT

...There was going to be a march and a demonstration. I thought carefully for a moment or two, then decided to participate, driving my car past the hundreds of students marching down to the big parking lot where the rally was to be held... I stayed in my car during the rally, listening intently to each speaker and cheering and shouting with the crowd.

The POWs

As in other conflicts, both sides took prisoners of war (POWs). The South Vietnamese held both **Viet Cong** and NVA troops, while the **communists** took ARVN and Americans as prisoners. In the USA, naturally, the media and the government focused on US POWs as well as troops listed as missing in action (MIA).

The first US POWs were members of the Special Forces, the advisers sent to aid the South Vietnamese. Later, air force and navy pilots shot down over North Vietnam made up the bulk of the POWs. Often found by hostile civilians, many of the pilots went to a Hanoi prison. The Americans nicknamed it 'the Hanoi Hilton', after the famous hotel chain. About 800 Americans were taken as POWs, while almost two thousand more were MIA.

Life as a POW
John McCain was a US Navy pilot taken prisoner in 1967. He was held as a POW for over five years. Later, he entered politics and served as a US senator. He also ran for president in the 2000 election. In this interview, he describes some of his experiences as a POW.

A 1949 international agreement called the Geneva Convention outlined the treatment POWs should receive in captivity. North Vietnam had signed the agreement, but it ignored many of its requirements. (The South Vietnamese did as well.) The North Vietnamese and the Viet Cong often tortured American POWs or forced them to stay in tiny bamboo cages. The communists also used them for their **propaganda**, to try to convince their own people and foreigners that they were winning the war.

A young North Vietnamese woman trains a gun on a US pilot shot down near Hanoi in 1967. Most American POWs were captured pilots.

A group of Vietnamese . . . pulled me into shore. The crowd was very hostile. They began kicking and beating me... It was pretty tense and the army people came up, put me into a truck, took me to the Hanoi Hilton. I was in very bad shape so it didn't take a lot of interrogating. They would slap me a few times and I would go in and out of consciousness. But it was clear to me that they didn't provide medical treatment unless we gave military information.

I was on the floor of the cell for about four or five days with a blanket over me. One day the guard came in with one of his friends, pulled the blanket up. My knee was the size and shape and color of a football. I told him, I said, 'Get the interrogator.' The interrogator came in and I said, 'Look, take me to the hospital, give me some treatment and then maybe we can talk about military information.'... Some hours later . . . the door opened and the interrogator said, 'Your father is a big admiral and we're going to take you to the hospital.' So the fact that my father was an admiral in the navy saved my life.

President Richard Nixon greets former POW John McCain after his release from North Vietnam in 1973 after five and a half years in captivity.

Turning points

By the end of 1967, President Lyndon Johnson faced heavy criticism for the war in Vietnam. The president's problems increased after 30 January 1968, when the **communists** launched the **Tet** offensive. Using hidden weapons and fighters, they launched a series of surprise attacks in South Vietnamese cities. Thousands of South Vietnamese civilians were massacred, including 2800 in the city of Hue (see page 51). The **Viet Cong** and NVA themselves lost thousands of their best troops. Tet, however, had a positive result for the north. More Americans now sensed that the USA was losing the war, even though US officials had been telling them the opposite. Johnson's support fell even more, and in March he decided not to seek re-election.

A few months after Tet, US troops raided the village of My Lai, looking for Viet Cong. Without being fired on, the soldiers massacred more than 400 civilians – women, children and old men. The US government tried to keep the attack secret, but in 1969, Americans learned about the 'My Lai Massacre'. Many were horrified about US soldiers acting so cruelly. A commander on the scene that day, Lieutenant William Calley, was later **court-martialled** for killing 22 civilians. My Lai became a symbol for all that was wrong about the Vietnam War.

This scene shows the once-beautiful, ancient city of Hue, where about 70 per cent of the houses were destroyed during the communist Tet offensive, 1968. Thousands of civilians were killed.

Choosing not to kill

Hugh Thompson Jr. was a helicopter pilot at My Lai who tried to stop some of the killing. In 1998, in a computer chat session with the Cable News Network (CNN), he described his actions during the massacre.

It was clear to us that something was going wrong. And at one time we had asked for assistance on a wounded civilian and a captain walked up and shot the girl we'd asked assistance for. Another time, we'd seen an irrigation ditch full of bodies, of which some were still living. We landed and talked to the Americans on the ground, said there are some wounded civilians in the ditch, can you help them out. And we were told, yes, we'll help them out of their misery. I said, quit joking, how 'bout helping them, and they said OK. As I took off, they walked to the ditch, and we heard machine-gun fire… Shortly after then, we saw some Vietnamese who had just made it to a bunker and were hiding inside the bunker. On the other side of the opening, we saw the American forces coming toward them. We just kind of figured those people were dead in about 15 seconds if we didn't do something. That's when we elected to land the aircraft between the American forces and the bunker… The things that went wrong that day were poor leadership, peer pressure and prejudice.

In 1971, Lt. William Calley (centre) was sentenced to life in prison for his role in the My Lai Massacre. This sentence was later reduced to ten years; he served one-third of this time before winning his release.

Nixon's war

Just before the 1968 presidential election, Lyndon Johnson almost worked out a deal with North Vietnam to end the war – until South Vietnamese leader Nguyen Van Thieu refused to go along. Thieu had been in contact with representatives of Richard Nixon, the Republican candidate. Nixon encouraged Thieu to wait, saying he would offer better peace terms to South Vietnam if he were elected.

Nixon did win, and he promised Americans a new approach to defeating the **communists** in Vietnam and ending US involvement. He began a policy called Vietnamization: the USA sent more military aid (money and weapons, backed by US air power) to South Vietnam, so their own troops could do more of the fighting. At the same time, he began bringing home US forces.

Nixon also increased bombing of North Vietnam and started bombing communist bases in Cambodia. Technically, Cambodia was neutral, but its leaders knew the North Vietnamese and **Viet Cong** were operating in their country. Fearing protests from both **Congress** and the public, Nixon kept the Cambodian bombings secret. By May 1969, however, the US press learned of the attacks. The next spring, US ground forces also attacked Cambodia. Meanwhile, Vietnamization continued – more than 100,000 troops had come home since Nixon had taken office.

The Vietnam War was the major issue in the 1968 presidential election, when former US vice president Richard Nixon, a Republican, defeated then-vice president Hubert Humphrey.

This is not an invasion of Cambodia. The areas in which these attacks will be launched are completely occupied and controlled by North Vietnamese forces. Our purpose is not to occupy the areas. Once enemy forces are driven out of these sanctuaries and once their military supplies are destroyed, we will withdraw...

Now, let me give you the reasons for my decision.

A majority of the American people, a majority of you listening to me, are for the withdrawal of our forces from Vietnam. The action I have taken tonight is indispensable for the continuing success of that withdrawal program...

We take this action not for the purpose of expanding the war into Cambodia, but for the purpose of ending the war in Vietnam and winning the just peace we all desire. We have made and we will continue to make every possible effort to end this war through negotiation at the conference table rather than through more fighting on the battlefield...

If, when the chips are down, the world's most powerful nation, the United States of America, acts like a pitiful, helpless giant, the forces of totalitarianism and anarchy will threaten free nations and free institutions throughout the world.

A distracted president

In the USA, new **demonstrations** followed the invasion of Cambodia. On 4 May 1970, at Kent State University, Ohio, National Guard troops killed four students, which led to even greater protests. The next year, Nixon faced a new problem at home: the release of the Pentagon Papers. This massive set of documents traced the history of the US role in **Indochina** from the end of World War II to 1968. The papers were never supposed to be made public, but Daniel Ellsberg, who worked at the Pentagon, gave them to reporters. Nixon was furious. Even though the Pentagon Papers dealt with policies shaped before he became president, Nixon did not want Americans to know the government had sometimes lied about its activities in Vietnam.

He feared the public might question his own statements and actions.

On 4 May 1970, protestors at Kent State flee as troops open fire, killing four people. At a demonstration at Jackson State, an African-American college in Mississippi, two more students were killed.

Nixon ordered his staff to investigate Ellsberg. The staff also made a long list of 'enemies' – celebrities and reporters who opposed Nixon and his policies. In 1972, the team in charge of these efforts ordered a secret burglary at the headquarters of the Democratic Party, the main rival of Nixon's Republican Party. The break-in took place at a Washington office complex called Watergate. Nixon began to focus more energy on trying to distance himself from the break-in and other illegal activities. The Watergate affair turned into the worst political scandal in US history and it eventually forced Nixon to resign in 1974.

Lies and secrets

Bob Haldeman worked as one of Richard Nixon's top aides. His diary gives us an insight into the president's response to the *New York Times'* printing of the Pentagon Papers in June 1971. Nixon lost his legal challenge to stop the *Times* from printing all of the papers.

Tuesday, June 15, 1971

The big thing today was still the *New York Times* story follow-up, as they go on running it and the whole thing builds. [US Attorney General John] Mitchell went ahead last night with his request of them to cease publication; they refused... After meeting with the P [Nixon] this afternoon, decided to file criminal charges. So we're pretty much in the soup on the whole thing now. The real problem is to try to establish clearly that the Administration's interest here is in the violation of Top Secret classifications rather than in the release of this particular material. The problem otherwise is that we're going to get tied into it and get blamed for the same kind of deception that was practiced by the Johnson Administration.

The P dictated a memo to me this morning, issuing orders that there is to be no contact . . . with the *New York Times* unless there is express permission from the P, which he does not intend to grant... He also felt that we should launch an attack on the *Times*; that it was a reckless disclosure of secrets and a shocking breach of security.

Talk of peace

Nixon's key aide on foreign relations was national security adviser Henry Kissinger. Starting in 1970, Kissinger held secret talks with both China and the Soviet Union, hoping to improve relations with those two **communist** nations. Nixon made historic trips to both countries in 1972, and the Soviets and the Chinese began to press the North Vietnamese to end the war.

The most productive peace talks began in September 1972. Kissinger met Le Duc Tho, a North Vietnamese **diplomat**, in Paris. The USA promised to leave **Indochina**. Thieu would remain president of South Vietnam and continue to receive US aid. The **Viet Cong** would also be allowed to stay in the south, and communists would have a role in the government there. For a while the talks broke down, and at Christmas, 1972, Nixon ordered the largest bombing raids of the war against North Vietnam. When the raids ended, the two sides agreed to the same terms they had reached earlier. Now, however, Thieu refused to accept the terms. With the threat of losing all US aid, Thieu finally gave in, accepting the presence of communists in the South. Nixon proclaimed that the USA had achieved 'peace with honour'.

How to get out?

In his 1979 book *White House Years*, Henry Kissinger explained some of his thinking as he tried to end the US military role in Vietnam.

The Nixon Administration entered office determined to end our involvement in Vietnam. But it soon came up against the reality that had also bedeviled [been a problem for] its predecessor. For nearly a generation the security and progress of a free people [the South Vietnamese] had depended on confidence in America. We could not simply walk away from an enterprise [the war] involving two administrations, five allied countries, and thirty-one thousand dead as if we were switching a television channel…

The domestic turmoil [agitation within the USA] of the Vietnam debate therefore pained me deeply. I did not agree with many of the decisions that had brought about the impasse [deadlock] in Indochina; I felt, however, that my appointment to high office entailed [included] a responsibility to help end the war in a way compatible with American self-respect and the stake that all men and women of goodwill had in America's strength and purpose. It seemed to me important for America not to be humiliated, not to be shattered, but to leave Vietnam in a manner that even the protesters might later see as reflecting an American choice made with dignity and self-respect… it was precisely the issue of our self-confidence and faith in our future that I considered at stake in the outcome in Vietnam.

An interpreter stands between Henry Kissinger (left) and Le Duc Tho (right) who worked out the agreement that ended the US involvement in the Vietnam War. The men shared the 1973 Nobel Peace Prize, which Tho rejected because his country was still at war.

Coming home

Many US soldiers had trouble adjusting to life at home when they returned from Vietnam. After past wars, returning US troops were treated as heroes. While some Americans did honour the returning veterans, anti-war protesters sometimes spat on them or called them 'babykillers'. Some of the soldiers also returned home with wounds that left them permanently disabled. Others had emotional scars. Over time, doctors discovered that many veterans had post-**traumatic** stress disorder (PTSD). After seeing friends killed and having killed enemy troops or Vietnamese civilians, some soldiers suffered from recurring nightmares, depression and physical ailments. Some veterans also came home addicted to drugs they had first used in Vietnam to escape the pressures of the war.

Good for some
Jim Noonan fought in Vietnam from September 1966 to October 1967. Unlike some veterans, he saw his experience in Vietnam as a positive influence on his life.

Vietnam veterans sometimes resented the treatment they received. Even after the last US troops left Vietnam in March 1973, many Americans felt guilty about the US role in **Indochina**. In 1982, however, the USA finally honoured the veterans, with the Vietnam Veterans Memorial in Washington, DC. A V-shaped granite wall features the names of all the 58,229 American men and women killed during the Vietnam War.

At a 1970 rally, construction workers show their continuing support for the Vietnam War and the soldiers fighting it. By this time, widespread American support for the war had declined sharply.

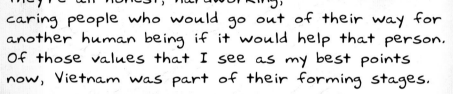

A veteran touches the names of his fallen comrades on the Vietnam Memorial in Washington, D.C. Today, people from around the world visit the memorial to pay their respects to the American men and women who died in Vietnam.

I believed that it was my duty to go to Vietnam. And that has to do with the values my parents instilled in me. I'd like to think that I have maintained those values, because they are good ones. I'm very proud of my family. They're all honest, hardworking, caring people who would go out of their way for another human being if it would help that person. Of those values that I see as my best points now, Vietnam was part of their forming stages.

I got through high school by the skin of my teeth. But after Vietnam, I went through college in three years on the dean's list [list of exceptional students]. Yet, it's hard to reflect upon a situation where so many have suffered and think about it in terms of what you personally have gained. But I do think that as a result of my military experience I am a stronger and more confident person. I also doubt that I'll ever be that scared again. I can always think, 'No matter what comes up, I'll know I've been more scared.'

. . . in Vietnam, there were a lot of guys who put their life on the line for their brothers, for principle, for whatever reasons they thought it was important. And it's in the moment when a person makes that decision that the effort really stands out.

The fall of Saigon

Under the 1973 peace treaty, North and South Vietnam agreed to a ceasefire, but the fighting soon resumed, as the North Vietnamese had no intention of giving up their fight to control the South. And until August 1973, the USA continued to bomb **communist** bases in Cambodia. During that summer, **Congress** decided that the US government would not spend more money to fight anywhere in **Indochina**. The USA as a whole was tired of the war and increasingly critical of Nixon, because of Watergate.

The **Viet Cong** slowly began to capture land under South Vietnamese government control. At the same time, South Vietnam faced economic troubles. The **refugees** in the cities lacked jobs and soldiers were going unpaid, while Thieu and his friends made money from **corruption**. The problems increased in 1974, when Congress cut $300 million from the money Nixon had promised Thieu.

In January 1975, the communists began their last major military campaign of the war. Within four months, they captured Saigon and took control of the South Vietnamese government. By this time, Cambodia was also ruled by local communists, and before the year's end Laos was under communist control as well. The US policy of containment had failed in Indochina.

South Vietnam refugees move south towards Saigon to escape the last communist assault.

Life after war

The North Vietnamese and Viet Cong celebrated the end of the war. Southerners, however, faced new difficulties. Thieu's corrupt government was replaced by communist leaders who often used brutal tactics to ensure loyalty to their cause. Tran Van Luu, who later left Vietnam, describes life during peacetime in Saigon.

On April 30, 1975, as the Communists took over Saigon, my neighbours were just wandering in the streets, very shocked. Crowds mutely stared at tanks rolling by, carrying militia wearing red armbands and shooting into the air. We did not know what to do...

At first people came into the streets to watch the North Vietnamese fighters out of curiosity. There was no voluntary **demonstration** to support the new government. We regarded the Communists as strangers, not heroes. But after a few weeks, when the Communists organized demonstrations, a lot of people came because we were scared.

After the collapse, I chose to remain in Saigon. My wife was teaching school and I had enough money saved to buy and sell things. But I became more and more afraid for my family because there were public executions. The Communists appointed a very tough major to maintain order. I saw with my own eyes people being executed near the theater on Truong Minh Giang Street, where I lived. In front of a crowd of people, including children, they shot a young boy, just twelve or thirteen years old...

For my wife and children, the school system changed drastically. Teachers identified as having commitment to the former **republic** were arrested. The Communist Party sent in new teachers from the North to take over the schools in Saigon... Arithmetic was formed around such destructive themes as: 'There are eight enemy helicopters in the sky; our victorious soldiers brought down six. How many are left?'

The refugees

After the Vietnam War, more than 2 million people fled **Indochina**. Some **refugees** did not want to live in a **communist** country. Others hoped to escape the violence that continued in the region. After 1975, the Communist government in Cambodia killed several million of its own people. A few years later, Vietnam tried to replace Cambodian leader Pol Pot with a leader who would support its interests, leading to a war between the countries. In 1979, China invaded Vietnam, as punishment for the Vietnamese attack on Cambodia and Vietnam's harsh treatment of its Chinese residents. That war destroyed parts of Vietnam that had escaped major damage during the war with the USA.

The first refugees were mostly former political and military leaders in South Vietnam. Over time, average citizens fled in greater numbers. Most refugees headed first for refugee camps in Thailand, the Philippines, Indonesia and Hong Kong. From there, the majority went on to the USA, Europe and Australia. To help the refugees, the USA changed its immigration laws, making it easier for South-east Asians to enter the country. By the mid-1990s, more than 1.25 million refugees had settled in America. Occasionally, the Asian immigrants faced discrimination in their new homes. Many Americans feared the refugees would take away jobs from US citizens or require large amounts of government aid. Over time, however, the fears over South-east Asian refugees have lessened, and many have prospered in America.

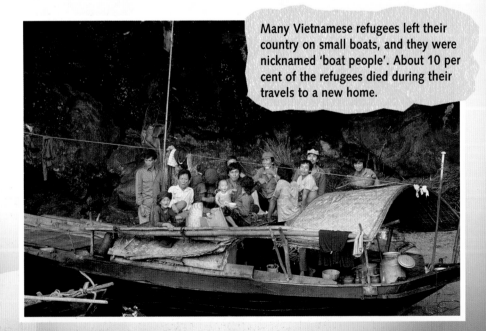

Many Vietnamese refugees left their country on small boats, and they were nicknamed 'boat people'. About 10 per cent of the refugees died during their travels to a new home.

We floundered on the high seas for nineteen days and nights, and then our boat was carried by the currents back to Vietnamese territorial waters. We didn't know where we were. We ran aground at Phu Quy Island in the province of Phan Thiet. During those nineteen days and nights we had been tortured by hunger and thirst. Many had died. Others had committed suicide by jumping overboard when they had become delirious with thirst. Most of us had drunk our own urine. We had been robbed five times by Thai fishing boats, but we had nothing. It was because of these pirates that we had survived, because they gave us drinking water, and rice broth. Not all pirates were killers. It is thanks to them that I am alive to write this to you today.

During our escape, I cheated death at least twice. My dear brother and sister, our attempt to seek freedom, to seek our family reunion, to look for a better future at the end, achieved nothing. Now, back in Vietnam, I have lost everyone and everything. . . My dear brother and sister, why did our maker punish me by giving me such misery?

These Vietnamese-American students are part of the large refugee population that settled in California and other states after the war.

Vietnam today

With its victory in 1975, Vietnam accomplished two major goals: independence and unity. The effects of the war, however, endure.

The economy is a major issue. The war destroyed industries and killed many young people who would have added to the country's wealth. Vietnam also faced US sanctions (restrictions on the goods Americans could buy from or sell to Vietnamese). These sanctions, which were not lifted until 1994, limited the growth of some Vietnamese industries. During the 1980s, the government began adopting some **capitalist** methods to strengthen the economy. In the mid-1990s Vietnam was caught up in the financial crisis that hit many Asian countries and the government, under the control of the **Communist** Party, lost confidence in this approach. Now, some cities, particularly in the south, bustle with activity and the country exports some goods, but about one-third of the Vietnamese still live in poverty.

Vietnam also faces the long-term effects of US weapons. The chemicals in **defoliants** such as Agent Orange are believed to have caused a high number of birth defects and other health problems. (Some US soldiers claim their health, too, was damaged by the defoliants.) The Vietnamese also face continuing danger from unexploded landmines set during the war.

In 1995, Vietnam and the USA established official relations for the first time. Several years later, the USA signed a trade treaty with the Vietnamese, who hoped the deal would continue economic growth. The country faces many years of hard work to help all its citizens prosper.

A Vietnamese mother holds her daughter, who suffers from birth defects possibly related to her father's exposure to Agent Orange during the war. Up to 1 million Vietnamese may have suffered from the effects of dioxin, a chemical in that defoliant.

A poet's perception

Pham Tien Duat, a Vietnamese poet, fought for North Vietnam during the war. In 1997, he offered some of his thoughts on how his people cope with their memories of the conflict.

The women, too, want to put the war behind them, to forget it but they can't. How can those hundreds of thousands of wives forget when their husbands were killed before they could ever have their first child, and now live the rest of their still young lives as widows? How can those thousands of children born deformed at birth forget? How can thousands of invalid veterans forget?

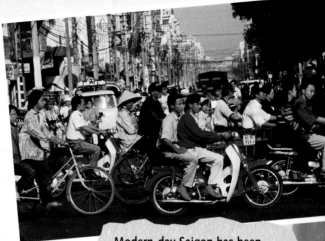

Modern-day Saigon has been renamed Ho Chi Minh City and commuters jam the busy streets instead of fleeing **refugees**.

And yet, to open a new and bright chapter between the US and Vietnam, it seems best if both sides close the door of the past. And rightly so, for hatred is neither good for others, nor for oneself. That sorrowful door to the past needs to be shut. But, in order to close a door, it's worthwhile to understand what it is that we close. Sadly, after over twenty years have passed since the war ended, many can still only vaguely see the contour of that door as if looking through a veil of mist.

I . . . have tried to write about the war, to describe and analyze it, but it still doesn't seem enough. It is as if I were standing in the midst of a crowd and calling out, but the noise makes it impossible for my friends to hear. There is therefore no choice but to call out once again, even if the voice becomes hoarse, until it is heard.

What have we learnt?

Through the words of both soldiers and civilians, this book has tried to show the reality of the Vietnam War – or wars. The Vietnamese actually fought two wars to win their independence, a 30-year struggle that cost several million lives. The US government played a key role from the beginning, hoping to stop the spread of **communism**. In the process, it supported a **corrupt** South Vietnamese government and lied to its own citizens. Many Americans felt betrayed, and their trust in their leaders was slow to return.

The North Vietnamese often said they would fight for years, if necessary, since they were fighting for their homeland. With their victory, they secured their communist rule in the south. Today, however, some Vietnamese – inside and out of the country – complain about the lack of **democracy** and freedom in Vietnam.

The Vietnam War had many lasting effects on both the victors and the defeated. Soldiers on both sides were crippled, and the war forced both sides to spend money on weapons that could have been used in other ways. In general, however, the civilians of Vietnam paid the highest price in casualties, while the survivors watched their homes and land destroyed.

The war also affected the spirit of both Vietnamese and Americans. US leaders decided that in the future, its military would not fight distant wars unless the USA had a clear interest at stake, and it was sure it could win. The Vietnam experience has sometimes caused American leaders to avoid sending troops to foreign nations or to do so reluctantly, as when war broke out in Yugoslavia during the 1990s. Yet when they do, some Americans say the government is repeating the mistakes of Vietnam, as some critics charged when the USA invaded Iraq in 2003. For the Vietnamese, the war restored their pride as an independent nation. Now, the two countries, once such bitter enemies, find ways to work together for the future.

A bombed out guard tower, along with other remnants of the war, remind the Vietnamese of their long struggle for independence.

Next day, we traveled north to Hue. I was surprised how the Citadel still bore the scars of Tet 1968 (see page 34). In fact, I almost expected to see a flak-jacketed Marine or sandal-clad **Viet Cong** jump from the dark recesses of a blown out building. Time had stood still in Vietnam, preserving one of the greatest battles of the war. Tru [Austin's guide] described the enemy's month-long occupation of the city, when thousands of Hue citizens were executed by the North Vietnamese for suspicion of being collaborators with the Saigon regime.

'They were shot, hung, hacked to death, burned or buried alive. Some were weighted down with stones and drowned in the river.'

Technically a communist and my former enemy, Tru was also one of the most decent and understanding men I could hope to meet. That evening, we sat quietly at the edge of the Perfume River in Hue, sipping beer as we watched the sun set on the western mountains. Tru joined me in a toast to the six Blue Ghosts, all from the scout platoon, who were killed there June 11 and 12, 1972.

Timeline

1945	The Viet Minh, led by Ho Chi Minh, declare Vietnamese independence from France.
1946	France bombards the city of Haiphong, triggering the first Vietnam War.
1950	President Harry Truman begins direct aid to France to help it fight the Vietnamese.
1954	With their victory at Dien Bien Phu, the Vietnamese win their war for independence; Vietnam is split in two along the **17th parallel**.
1955	Ngo Dinh Diem takes control in South Vietnam.
1959	North Vietnam begins armed revolt in the south, hoping to reunite Vietnam.
1961	President John F. Kennedy increases the number of US military advisers in South Vietnam from 900 to 3000.
1963	Diem is **assassinated** and replaced by a series of military leaders; Kennedy is assassinated and replaced by Lyndon Johnson; the number of US military personnel in South Vietnam reaches 16,000.
1964	Johnson uses a military incident in the Gulf of Tonkin to win approval from **Congress** for greater US military action in **Indochina**; bombing of Ho Chi Minh Trail in Laos begins.
1965	First heavy bombing of North Vietnam begins; first US combat troops arrive in South Vietnam; Battle of Ia Drang is first major clash between Americans and North Vietnamese.
1967	Major peace **demonstrations** across the USA; Nguyen Van Thieu becomes president of South Vietnam.
1968	**Tet** Offensive; Johnson decides not to seek re-election; supporters of Richard Nixon play role in ending peace talks; Nixon is elected president; US troops in Indochina reach more than 500,000.
1969	Nixon begins Vietnamization policy and brings home first US troops; bombing of Cambodia begins; My Lai Massacre takes place; Ho Chi Minh dies; more large anti-war protests in the USA.
1970	Nixon sends ground troops into Cambodia; six college students die in anti-war protests.
1971	Several newspapers publish the Pentagon Papers.
1972	Nixon visits both China and the Soviet Union; the Watergate break-in occurs; Henry Kissinger and Le Duc Tho conduct peace talks in Paris; Nixon orders massive bombing of North Vietnam at Christmastime.
1973	The USA and North Vietnam sign a peace treaty; US POWs are released and last American troops pull out of South Vietnam, but the war continues; Nixon faces questions about his role in Watergate.
1974	Congress cuts aid to South Vietnam; Nixon resigns.
1975	North Vietnam wins the Vietnam War; communist governments also come to power in Cambodia and Laos; **refugees** begin fleeing the region.
1982	The Vietnam Veterans Memorial opens in Washington, DC.
1995	The USA and Vietnam establish official diplomatic relations.

Find out more

Books & websites

Cold War: The Hot Conflicts Michael Burgan (Raintree Steck-Vaughn Publishers, 2001)
Vietnam Terri Willis (Children's Press, 2002)
The Vietnam War David Willoughby (Heinemann Library, 2001)

The American Experience: Vietnam Online
http://www.pbs.org/wgbh/amex/vietnam/intro.html
This website features transcripts of the television series *Vietnam: A History* as well as additional information about the war and the people who fought it.

Studying the Vietnam War Online
http://www.refstar.com/vietnam/online_study.html
A site featuring detailed links to the Vietnam War, including interviews and documents.

Communist Party of Vietnam
http://www.refstar.com/vietnam/online_study.html
This official party site has details on current government policies and information on Ho Chi Minh.

POTUS – Presidents of the USA
http://www.ipl.org/div/potus/
For information on the presidents who served during the Vietnam War.

List of primary sources

The author and publisher gratefully acknowledge the following publications from which written sources in the book are drawn. In some cases the wording or sentence structure has been simplified to make the material more appropriate for a school readership.

Page 9 Vietnamese Declaration of Independence, printed in Robert J. McMahon (ed.), *Major Problems in the History of the Vietnam War*, (D.C. Heath and Company, 1990)
Page 11 Interview in *Vietnam: A Television History*, PBS TV Series, 'Roots of a War' episode [available online at http://www.pbs.org/wgbh/amex/vietnam/101ts.html]
Page 13 John Foster Dulles speech to the Overseas Press Club, quoted in David Bender (ed.), *The Vietnam War: Opposing Viewpoints*, (Greenhaven Press, 1998)
Page 15 Interview 'The Underground School' in Al Santoli, *To Bear Any Burden*. (E.P. Dutton, Inc., 1985)
Page 17 Homer Bigart, 'A "Very Real War" in Vietnam—and the Deep U.S. Commitment' in *Reporting Vietnam Part One: American Journalism 1959-1969*, (The Library of America, 1998)
Page 19 Interview in Robert Steinman, *The Soldiers' Story: Vietnam in Their Own Words*, (TV Books, 1999)
Page 21 Interview in Martha Hess, *Then the Americans Came: Voices from Vietnam*, (Four Walls/Eight Windows, 1993)
Page 23 Testimony from the Winter Soldier Investigation, as printed in the Congressional Record,

April 7, 1971 and available online at the Sixties Project,
http://lists.village.virginia.edu/sixties/HTML_docs/Resources/Primary.html.

Page 25 Le Ly Hayslip, with Jay Wurts, *When Heaven and Earth Changed Places: A Vietnamese Woman's Journey from War to Peace*, (Doubleday, 1989)

Page 27 Interview in David Chanoff and Doan Van Toai, *Portrait of the Enemy*, (Random House, 1986)

Page 29 Richard Pyle, 'From Tonkin Gulf to Persian Gulf', CNN Cold War, available online at http://www.cnn.com/SPECIALS/cold.war/episodes/11/then.now.

Page 31 Ron Kovic, *Born on the Fourth of July*, (Pocket Books, 1976)

Page 33 Interview in Ron Steinman, *The Soldiers' Story*, (TV Books, 1999)

Page 35 Online chat with Hugh Thompson Jr., CNN Cold War, available at http://www.cnn.com/SPECIALS/cold.war/guides/debate/chats/thompson/

Page 37 Richard Nixon televised address, May 11, 1970, printed in Robert J. McMahon (ed.), *Major Problems in the History of the Vietnam War*, (D.C. Heath and Company, 1990)

Page 39 H. R. Haldeman, *The Haldeman Diaries: Inside the Nixon White House*, (G.P. Putnam's Sons, 1994)

Page 41 Henry Kissinger, *White House Years* (Little, Brown and Company, 1979)

Pages 43 and 45 Interviews in Al Santoli, *To Bear Any Burden*, (E.P. Dutton, 1985)

Page 47 Letter printed in Lesleyanne Hawthorne (ed). *Refugee: The Vietnamese Experience*, (Oxford University Press, 1982)

Page 49 Pham Tien Duat, 'The Vietnam War: Remember in Order to Forget', at Vietnam Online, http://www.pbs.org/wgbh/amex/vietnam/reflect/duat.html.

Page 51 Mike Austin, 'Closure: A Vietnam Story', Vietnam Veterans Homepage, available online at http://grunt.space.swri.edu/closure.htm.

Glossary

17ᵗʰ parallel line of latitude that served as the first border between North and South Vietnam

aggressors people who start military action against another group of people or country

ally state, organization or person that supports another

ambush hide and launch a surprise attack

archives collection of documents, sources or evidence

artillery large, mobile guns

assassination murder of a political figure

cadre a highly trained and active member of a political party or military force

capitalism economic system that uses private wealth to produce goods and services

censor remove words or ideas from a news report

civil rights nonpolitical rights, such as freedom and equality, which belong to a person because he or she is a citizen, and regardless of race, religion, colour or sex

classified secret

Cold War period of East-West tension, 1946-89, that stopped short of a hot (fighting) war

colonial relating to a colony, an area of land where political power and national resources are controlled by another country

communism political theory advocating a society in which all property and services are publicly owned and each person is paid and works according to his or her needs and abilities

Congress the highest law-making body of the USA

corrupt   dishonest; open to bribery
court-martialled   tried in a military court for an offence against military law
declassified   formerly secret but now open
defoliant   chemical that kills plants and trees
demilitarized zone   area where weapons are not allowed
democratic   practising democracy: a system of government in the which the governed – the people – periodically choose their governors in free elections. Genuinely democratic states uphold human rights and freedoms
demonstrations   large protests usually against a government or its policies, but sometimes in favour of them
diplomat   someone representing one nation who talks to the representatives of another; not a military person
draft   process for selecting troops to serve in the military
guerrilla war   fighting style that relies on small unofficial forces that hide and then quickly strike an enemy
ideological   relating to a set of basic beliefs that shape attitudes and actions
imperialism   political and military system focused on taking over other countries or influencing their governments
Indochina   part of South-east Asia that includes Cambodia, Laos and Vietnam

napalm   jelly-like form of petrol that burns on contact
nationalism   efforts to end foreign influence or control of one's homeland
nuclear weapons   devices that use the energy inside atoms to create large explosions
press conferences   meetings held by government officials to give information to news reporters
propaganda   information spread by a country or organization to influence others' beliefs or actions in specific way
refugees   civilians who flee their homes because of war or natural disasters
republic   a nation whose head of state is not a king or queen but a president
siege   military tactic of surrounding enemy forces so they cannot move or easily obtain supplies
stockades   simple prisons or forts built out of wood
Tet   the Vietnamese New Year, celebrated in January or February
traumatic   deeply disturbing
Viet Cong   communist South Vietnamese guerilla fighters
West   collective name for countries that share democratic political systems and capitalist economic systems; includes the USA, Canada, and most of the countries of Europe

Appendix

Other nations that aided South Vietnam and the USA during the Vietnam War, as part of the Free World Military Forces:
Australia
New Zealand
The Philippines
South Korea
Taiwan (advisers only)
Thailand
In addition, more than 30 countries provided aid to South Vietnam, including Brazil, Canada, Israel, Japan, Pakistan, Turkey and the United Kingdom.

Index